Ten Thousand Leaves

Ten   Thousand

SHAMBHALA

Leaves

Love Poems from the *Manyōshū*

Translated from the Japanese by Harold Wright

BOULDER   1979

SHAMBHALA PUBLICATIONS, INC.
1123 Spruce Street
Boulder, Colorado 80302

Translation © 1979 Harold Wright
All Rights Reserved

Distributed in the United States by Random House
and in Canada by Random House of Canada Ltd.

LIBRARY OF CONGRESS CATALOGING IN PUBLICATION DATA

Man'yoshu. English. Selections.
  Ten thousand leaves.

  1. Waka—Translations into English.
2. Love poetry, Japanese—Translations into
English. 3. English poetry—Translations from
Japanese. 4. Love poetry—Translations from Japanese.
I. Wright, Harold, 1931-   II. Title.

PL758.15.A28 1979   895.6'1'1   78-65436
ISBN 0-87773-151-9   ISBN 0-394-73690-7 (Random House)

Printed in the United States of America

These translations are dedicated with love to my daughters,
Larina and Rose

ACKNOWLEDGMENTS

I would like to express thanks to Robin Skelton for permission to reprint poems 1-11, 13-16, and 18-23, which first appeared in *The Malahat Review*, No. 21, January 1972, University of Victoria, Victoria, British Columbia, Canada; and to the Asia Society of New York for use of poems 44, 45, 53, 54, 76, 77, 100, 104, 130, and 136, which appeared in my article "The Poetry of Japan," *Asia*, No. 16, Autumn 1969, New York. I am also grateful to Roger F. Hackett, Acting Director of the Center for Japanese Studies, The University of Michigan, for a travel grant that permitted me to utilize the Japanese language materials at their Asia Library, and to a number of people at Ohio State University, especially Nancy Minson, Patches Eisenberg, and Lucy Bass, who were all very helpful in transforming my original jottings into readable English. I would like to express my deep appreciation, too, to Professor Robert Turoff of Antioch, who willingly took time from his teaching and research of theoretical physics to pose me here and there for a photograph. I am also indebted to Sora Newman of Columbus, who, through her deep appreciation of these poems and her aesthetic sensibilities, has been most helpful in editing and in working out the final format. To Professor Donald Keene I wish to express my deepest gratitude. His enduring encouragement has sustained me.

INTRODUCTION

The *Manyōshū* "needs no apologies," Donald Keene writes in the introduction to his *Anthology of Japanese Literature*. "It is one of the world's great collections of poetry."[1] The title of this outstanding work, *Manyōshū*, translates literally as "A Collection of Ten Thousand Leaves," but through implication *Manyōshū* can also mean "A Collection for Myriad Ages." Compiled in its final form during the eighth century, the anthology contains 4,516 poems arranged in twenty volumes. Embodying strength of feeling, sincerity, and simplicity, these poems have been honored as the purest expression of the early Japanese spirit.

Much of the *Manyōshū*'s richness is derived from the varied backgrounds of its over four hundred known contributors, not to mention the innumerable anonymous poets whose work is included in the collection. Noble sentiments of those residing in the court are found next to the rustic expressions of frontier guards stationed at lonely outposts. Folk songs, poems in praise of saké, longer poems on legendary themes, and even bawdy pieces find a place beside scenic descriptions and reflective poems. Whole sections of the work deal with the recurring themes of love's sensuality and spirituality, and the sorrow of separation.

Poetry was a basic form of communication between lovers, who were not always permitted to meet as frequently or as openly as they might have wished. The theme of separation persists throughout the poetry of early Japan, and indeed contemporary readers may be left with the feeling that early Japanese lovers spent more time apart than together. Instead of a more direct expression of the pleasurable joys of love, the poetic communications of the time seem to dwell on the sadness of "longing for love."

In this early period Japan was growing, under the cultural influence of China, into a more solidified nation-state in which the family was becoming a rigid social unit. Once the imperial family had

1. Keene, Donald, *Anthology of Japanese Literature*. New York: Grove Press, 1955.

established itself, in terms of divine and secular power, as the central-
ized authority of the island nation, marriage was openly used as a
political device to aid other powerful families or clans to move
further upwards toward the ultimate source of imperial power.
Having a daughter married to the emperor was the ambition of
many aristocrats, for in this way a man might see his own grandson
ascend the throne. "Marriage politics" can be seen as a vestige of
an earlier time in which the youth of various clans were traded as
hostages in an attempt to solidify and to unify power among the
struggling families. Consequently, men and women often were not
permitted to marry or to have open relationships with those most
attractive to them for fear of jeopardizing, not only their own
names, but the shaky political unions of the time. "Gossip," then,
was not merely the idle amusement of the leisure class; a scandle
could lead to the downfall of the holders of power.

Within the love poems themselves, references can be found to
leaving one's own legal wife in the pre-dawn hours for fear of being
seen. Perhaps due to Japan's matriarchal past, men and women,
even though officially married, lived in separate dwellings. Japan,
during the eighth century, was moving towards a more patriarchal
model, but it would be centuries before the Japanese woman would
be forced to surrender title, name, and home in marriage with a man
and his family not of her own choosing. Women of the *Manyōshū*
were still independent enough to retain their own identities and
residences. These aristocratic women did not, however, live alone.
Extended family and groups of ladies-in-waiting lived and slept in
collective units. Prying eyes were everywhere. Confucian morality
put pressure on women to remain chaste and faithful, but that con-
fining philosophy never made many inroads into the sexual mores
of the Japanese man. The *Manyō* male lover, at least, was probably
seeing several women in addition to his wife or wives, and he certainly didn't want the ladies to know too clearly where he spent
each night, when they were having to "pass the long nights alone."

Some ancient Japanese documents suggest that the Japanese love
poem sprang out of occasional songfests associated with Shinto
fertility rites of the distant past. At designated times the young
people in a community would be permitted to go off to a hillside
or to the grounds of a Shinto shrine to woo one another with song.
By the eighth century, however, such carefree evenings of song and
love were being condemned, at least in court circles, and only the
man was free to roam the streets in "longing for love." After the
popularization, too, of a writing system initially borrowed from

China, it was the song or poem alone that remained from the song-fest past. Spontaneous songs of a former period of history were transformed by the literate society of the eighth century into composed written statements of desire. But Confucian imposed morality was not the single reason for the persistent theme of separation in the love poetry of the day. At the time of the movement towards nation-state politics, there were whole areas of Japan where the "barbarians" had not yet come under complete control of the Nara Court. Wars and military occupations of disputed territory were still being carried out in the hinterlands. Frontier guards were continually being sent out to hold or to conquer territory. Many poems of longing or separation were written between these men and their women at home. Poem 41 in this volume is one example:

> We have received
> our Imperial Orders
> and from tomorrow
> We will sleep among the reeds
> while our wives remain behind

Many of the *Manyōshū* love poems selected for this present collection were written in and around the capitol city of Nara, and many of the individual poems were either written to or by one man, Ōtomo Yakamochi (716-785), who is believed by some scholars to have actually compiled the anthology. His influence in the *Manyōshū* was certainly important—in more than one way. His own aunt, Lady Ōtomo of Sakanoé (dates unknown) seems to have been involved romantically with him. In poem 89 she says:

> Since you did not come
> by the time the moon of pearl
> had fully risen
> I had then to dream of you
> to give you the love I felt

Later, Yakamochi became involved with his cousin, the above lady's daughter, and eventually married her. She is known only as "Lady Ōtomo of Sakanoé's Elder Daughter" (dates unknown). She wrote, apparently one lonely night, poem 13:

> Mist drifts in layers
> over Mt. Kasuga's crest
> yet the lovely moon
> Dimly glows all through the night
> and I must sleep alone

Perhaps, through gossip, this wife may have learned of the affair between her husband and a Lady Ki (dates unknown) who addressed the popular Yakamochi with similar sentiments in poem 8:

> If the night is dark
> you won't visit me, of course,
> but when the plum
> Is in bloom beneath the moon
> won't you come to be with me?

Perhaps, too, the wife may have suspected Lady Kasa (dates unknown) who has over twenty pleas for Yakamochi's attention recorded in the *Manyōshū*. He, however, only replied to her poetry twice. On one occasion, she, seeming to give up on the one-sided affair, wrote in poem 132:

> To love someone
> who does not return that love
> is like offering prayers
> Back behind a starving god
> within a Buddhist temple

The love poems in this volume were all written originally in the *tanka* (also called *waka*), which is a thirty-one syllable form subdivided into five units of five, seven, five, seven, and seven syllables respectively. Other forms of poetry were included in the *Manyōshū*, such as the thirty-eight syllable *sedōka* (divided into units of five, seven, seven, five, seven, and seven syllables respectively) and occasionally the much longer *choka* (made up of units of five and seven syllables that could alternate in up to one hundred lines, ending with a final couplet of seven, seven syllables). It was the thirty-one syllable *tanka*, however, that came to be the preferred form, especially as a medium for communicating love, and it is the only form of the three that remained popular beyond the eighth century. Along with the later seventeen syllable *haiku*, the *tanka* is still used today.

In the present translations an attempt is made to approximate the original syllabics of the eighth-century poems. Not all lines have been made up of rigidly structured groupings of five or seven syllables, however. In making the translation the flow of an individual line or group of lines has been given more importance than the mathematical tabulation of sounds.

The format of the original *Manyōshū* collection did not follow an organized or thematic plan, such as characterizes the later imperial collections of Japanese poetry. These anthologies of the tenth through the thirteenth centuries were arranged to provide a poetic sequence ordered by association and progression. Following the spirit of this model, without rigidly adhering to its elaborate rules, the poems in this volume have been arranged in a thematic sequence.

Harold Wright
Yellow Springs, Ohio

Love Poems from the
MANYOSHU

詠月

宇宙影不念物于此月之過邊春情夕
さ しもつ モノ コノ半 かん さも
サもつスモ ノ コノ羊 ニシニ半君

香宮
かも

石更し遊超借高之野邊削清照
ニえうり 上え カる 多ノノ へ サ ニ き りそれ
ニえうり 乃

月夜可閑
半ヨ かも

1.

Let us not cease
    to enjoy ourselves in drink,
        since the plants and trees
Which burst to bud in springtime
    will but wither in the fall

2.

Your favorite flowers
    that are growing near the house
        have bloomed and faded
Yet, the tears that fill my eyes
    have not begun to dry

3.

On the hill near home
    flowers of the fall bush clover
        will soon be scattered
How I wish she'd seen them now
    before they're harmed by the wind

4.

The flowers of the plum
    were covered with fallen snow
      which I wrapped up
But when I tried to have you see
    it was melting in my hands

5.

The sun of spring
    has melted the snow away
      likewise, your heart
Must have melted entirely
    since no message comes from you

6.

When spring arrives
    the frost on the river's moss
      is melted away
In such a way my heart melts
    over longing for your love

7.

Near my loved one's house
  there is now in full bloom
    a flowering plum tree
If it ever gives forth fruit
  then I will know what to do

8.

If the night is dark
  you won't visit me, of course,
    but when the plum
Is in bloom beneath the moon
  won't you come to be with me?

9.

Once I did believe
    that no love could still linger
      within my heart
Yet, a love springs from somewhere
    and forces itself on me

10.

Loving you, my lord,
    and giving way to longing
      I have come to you
Not knowing if the spring rain
    has ceased or still is falling

11.

The mountains in spring
    are as brightly colored
      as the waterfall
And my thoughts of love for you
    equal this profuse confusion

12.

This body of mine
    has crossed the mountain barrier
      and is here indeed!
But this heart of mine remains
    drawing closer to my wife

13.

Mist drifts in layers
    over Mt. Kasuga's crest
      yet the lovely moon
Dimly glows all through the night
    and I must sleep alone

14.

The rains of spring
    have not ceased to fall all day
      so I took shelter.
On the road to my love's home
    I have to wait in darkness

15.

As I pass before
    the house of the one that I love
      I wish only that
She would let me see her eyes
    even though we may not speak

16.

The moon crossed the sky
   and I saw him only once
     in its pale light
Yet, the person whom I saw
   does appear to me in dreams

17.

During your journey
   if you spend the night on shore
     and the mists rise up
Please know that it is my breath
   as it heaves forth in sighs

18.

Like the mists of spring
   that lie in distant layers
     over the mountains
I have seen you vaguely once
   but my love shall linger long

19.

Not a day goes by
    in which the mist does not rise
        on Mt. Kasuga
Likewise it is you, my lord,
    whom I long to see each day

20.

My eyes have seen you
    but I've yet to hold you close
        you're like the laurel
That is growing on the moon
    and I don't know what to do

21.

When spring arrives
    the shrike dives into the grass
        and goes in hiding
You too are unseen, my love,
    yet I gaze towards your home

22.

When the tide is full
  the surf covers up the shore
    hiding the seaweed
So like you the less I see
  the deeper grows my longing

23.

Her voice sings
    like a bird beneath the leaves
      of a fall mountain
If she'd only speak to me
    what would we have to grieve?

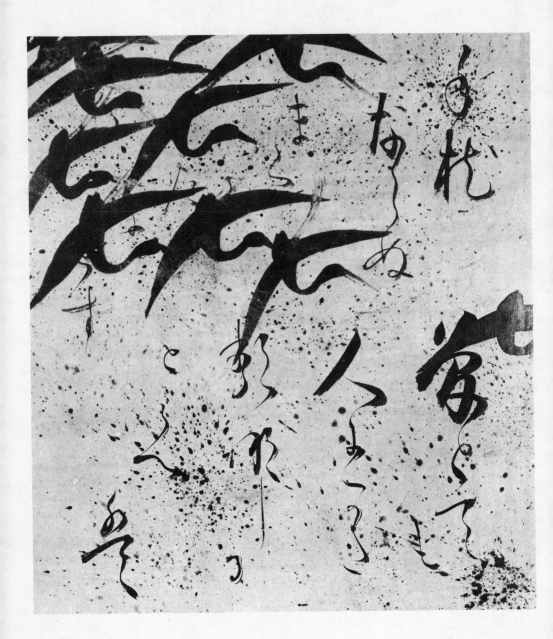

24.

Near these hot springs
    cranes are crying in a field
    and I wonder if
Like myself they long for love
    and weep unmindful of time

25.

Ah, if she were here
    we could listen together
    on this ocean shore
To the sound of passing cranes
    crying in the rising sun

26.

Like the crane that cries
    merely to be heard afar
    in the dark of night
Must I only hear from you?
    Will we never get to meet?

28.

The wind from the sea
　　blew strongly towards the shore
　　　　but to please my love
My sleeves became soaking wet
　　cutting seaweed for her sake

27.

Even the wild duck
　　that swims along the shores
　　　　of Lake Karu
Does not have to sleep alone
　　on a stretch of drifting moss

29.

It was in a dream
    that I saw a long straight sword
        lying at my side
I wonder what has been foretold
    perhaps you will visit me

30.

Going out to sea
    and sailing along the coast
        I hope to please you
By catching from the seaweed
    a carp of sword-handle size

31

31.

Just at break of day
    when I'm longing for my home
        there comes from the shore
The sounds of someone rowing—
    perhaps it's fishing girls!

32.

As I walk along
    the seashore at Naniwa
        young fishing girls
Gather in seaweed for food
    and I call and ask their names

33.

Please consider us
    merely as fishing girls
        and continue on. . . .
You're a traveler far from home
    and we can't reveal our names

34.

Since we are alone
  just you and I, my husband,
   what does it matter
If the moon does not appear
  due to high hills all around?

35.

I look back at her
  and wave my sleeves in parting
   from between the trees
Praying the clouds won't cover
  the moon that has just appeared

36.

When you left my side
  it was hard to see your face
   in the early dawn
So this lengthy day of spring
  will be spent in longing

37.

The mist has remained
  during this long day in spring
  and I felt longing
But when the full darkness falls
  I will come to visit you

38.

If the law were such
  that one always had to die
  because of love
It would be one thousand times
  I died only to return

39.

When I hear the news
  that your ship has entered
  the Bay of Naniwa
I will run out to meet you
  without tying up my sash!

40.

We face each other
    from the opposing shores
        of the Milky Way
When you come to me, my lord,
    do plan to undo your sash

41.

We have received
    our Imperial Orders
        and from tomorrow
We will sleep among the reeds
    while our wives remain behind

42.

This journey of mine
    I feel is but a journey
        but there at home—
Left to cling to the children—
    my wife grows thin in sorrow

43.

The cock is crowing
    as the men of the Eastlands
        take leave of their wives
Oh, the sadness that they feel
    seeing that long thread of years

44.

The time has come
    for me once more to return
      to the capital
But whose sleeves await me there
    to pillow my head in sleep?

45.

I'll give you my gown
    that is spread where we loved
      for your memories
Roll it round your white pillow
    to cushion your head in sleep

46.

This gown of yours
    given to me in memory
      of our love tonight
Will remain with me always
    even though it does not plead

47.

In the bamboo grass
    frost has fallen for the night
      and the robes I wear
Are heaped on me sevenfold
    Ah! the skin of my beloved!

48.

These traveling robes
    are piled eight high above me
      as I lie asleep
Yet, my skin still feels the cold—
    my wife is not beside me

49.

On a grass pillow
    you will sleep in traveling robes
      and your sash may tear—
As to sew it up yourself
    please take this needle with you!

50.

"Quickly return
    without harm from your journey"
      were my wife's words
But the sash she bound for me
    now has become so soiled!

51.

If I would have dyed
    the garments of my husband
      in a vivid hue
When he crossed that awesome slope
    I could have seen him clearly

52.

Longing for a love
    that I can no longer see
      I spread my robes
On the shore of Tama Bay
    where I'll have to sleep alone

54.

The cicada cries
everyday at the same hour
but I'm a woman
Much in love and very weak
and can cry anytime

53.

I am all alone
and feel the deepest sadness
but for condolence
I have come outside to hear
the crying of cicadas

55.

The sleet is falling
  on and on in my garden
    and the night is cold
Without a pillow of your arms
  I shall have to sleep alone

56.

The temple bell
  rings out saying, "go to sleep"
    for all to hear
Yet, I long so much for you
  I cannot close my eyes

57.

Here near our home
I gaze at needles of pine
as I pine for you
Hurry and return to me
so I won't die in longing

58.

At times I wonder
if people in the ancient past
like myself tonight
Found it difficult to sleep
due to longing over love

59.

It is not these days
alone that this holds true
in those former times
Lovers even went so far
as to weep in grief aloud

60.

The tears that I weep
    make me see the shining sun
        as complete darkness
Though they wet the robes I wear
    there's no one here to dry them

61.

In the sixth month
    the earth is caused to crack
        by the burning sun
Yet my sleeves are always wet
    when we do not get to meet

62.

They plowed a field
    on the shore of Suminoé
        and set out rice plants
Now the rice has all been reaped
    but I've yet to see you once

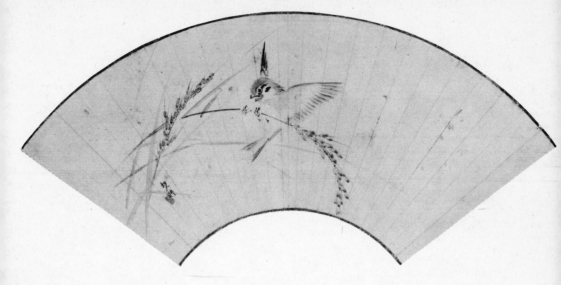

63.

Other men planted
    while you failed to plant your fields
        and so here again
You are traveling from your land
    and I wonder what I'll do

64.

I saddle my horse
    and ride out to see my love
        and when I begin
To ascend Mt. Ikoma
    the maple leaves are falling

65.

While I wait for you
    with longing in my breast
      back here at home
My bamboo blinds are fluttered
    by the blowing autumn breeze

66.

Off in the distance
    there I see my loved one's home
      on the horizon
How I long to be there soon
    get along black steed of mine!

67.

From Furu Mountain
    I can look directly down
      and see the capital
But I lie awake in longing
    even though you're nearer now

68.

The moon has risen
    to that predetermined point
        and she is thinking:
The time has come to go outside
    and wait for his arrival

69.

Even the breeze
    increases painful longing
        even the breeze
But I know that he will come
    so why feel grief in waiting?

70.

On a hill near home
    a young stag has come to cry
        in a field of clover
Searching for his mate through flowers
    there comes crying a young stag

71.

Over Uda's plain
    there comes thrashing a wild stag
        through autumn clover
He is longing for his mate
    but no more than I do mine

72.

From the high mountain
    the sound of a crying stag
        carries down valleys
How inspiring is his voice
    like yours, my loving lord

53

73.

A stag also calls
    to its mate on the same day
      I cross these mountains
Oh, my love, do you believe
    we will merely meet again?

74.

Through fields of autumn
    nothing's left to tell the trail
      of a stag at dawn
Though you felt the same, my lord,
    we have met again tonight

75.

When evening comes
    the stag on Mt. Ogura
      can be heard to cry
But perhaps he's still tonight
    After meeting with his mate

76.

If I do leave her
   I wonder if she will still
      have feelings for me
While her silken raven hair
      spreads about her through the night

77.

Everyone at home
    feeling that my hair's too long
      tells me to bind it
But it's as you saw it last
      though now a little tangled

78.

Although a warrior
   I am lying and weeping here
     while I make for you
A comb of willow branch
    let it adorn your hair

79.

This yellow rose
   has been grown with much care
     and here remains—
Yet, when you appear my love
   it will adorn your hair

80.

After you leave me
   I will not make up myself
     or even think
To take from my toilet case
   my set of boxwood combs

81.

Here on my journey
   I light a lamp in darkness
     such is my life
But my wife must live in gloom
   as she continues longing

82.

That wife of mine
　　longs painfully for me
　　　　but in my water
I see her form as I drink
　　and I know I can't forget

83.

A flying squirrel
　　sits up high in a treetop
　　　　of Mt. Mikuni
There he waits for passing birds
　　I too grow thin from longing!

84.

The autumn wind
　　will be blowing coldly
　　　　from now on
I wonder how I'll manage
　　to pass the long nights alone

85.

The leaves of autumn
    now have faded all away
        though my wife at home
Said she'd wait for my return
    this season too has gone

86.

The red leaves of oak
    in the plain of Inami
        appear in season
Yet, this longing for my love
    does not have seeds in time

87.

The mist of autumn
    rises up on this dark night
        and very faintly
Just as though it were a dream
    I see my love appear

88.

Upon the waves
   I spent the night afloat
      but what were her thoughts
To make her be as passionate
    as I saw her in my dreams?

89.

Since you did not come
    by the time the moon of pearl
    had fully risen
I had then to dream of you
    to give you the love I felt

90.

Having dreamt of you
    I felt so very saddened
    when I awoke
Searching for you at my side
    but I couldn't find your hand

91.

In your poem you say
    you will have to sleep alone
    on these long nights
But the one who went away
    will return in memories

92.

Should I sleep alone
    in my lonely empty home
    in the capital
How much worse it must be
    than all my nights of travel

93.

The drizzling rain
    falls and causes to drop off
    the leaves of autumn
My bed quilts are very cold
    and I have to sleep alone

94.

Wet by autumn rain
    that continues to fall
        in this wretched place
It is your house, my beloved,
    that never leaves my mind

95.

Like the morning mist
    that hovers over the heads of grain
      in the autumn fields
When will longing for my love
    lift up and be blown away?

96.

Through the evening mist
    there flies a flock of wild geese
      toward my loved one's home
They are calling as they fly
    and envy fills my heart

97.

Hidden by the mist
    that dimly veils the dawn
      the wild geese cry
Please take with you as you leave
    some words of love to my wife

98.

Who is there that heard
   the voice of the wild goose
      as it flew above?
Crying as he sought his mate
   oh, what a wondrous sound!

99.

You, my love, have asked
   if I heard the wild goose cry
      though I'm sure you know
The wild goose that cried above
   is hidden by distant clouds

100.

Wild geese are crying
　　while flying above the clouds
　　　　but they will settle
As thickly on the fields of grain
　　as the love I feel for you

101.

You are as distant
　　as the wild geese that fly
　　　　high above the clouds
But I longed for you so much
　　that I trudged along this far

102.

Do not even ask
    for I do not know the name
      of the man I love
Yet, for him I stand and wait
    all wet from the autumn dew

103.

Rather than to love
    in a town where gossip's thick
      I would much rather
Fly away with the wild geese
    which I hear cry this morning

104.

Even if gossip
    is as thick as the grasses
      in a summer field
So what if my love and I
    have slept entwined together

105.

There'll be so many
    nights that we will be together
       so please tell me why
Everyone is so upset
    over one night that we met

106.

When one is in love
    yet allows no one to know
       she must suffer so
But bloom like the flowering pink
    and every morning I will call

107.

This land is known
    to be extremely dreadful
       for its constant gossip
So don't let blushing betray love
    even in the face of death

108.

Is there somewhere
    a land where no one lives?
      Ah, to such a place
Hand in hand my love and I
    would go and live together

109.

On a hill in fall
    the leaves of trees are turning
      when touched by frost
But even though the years may pass
    I will never forget you

110.

Had I but known
    the direction that she'd take
      before she went away
I would have built a barrier
    that would have blocked her path

111.

How could I undo
    the sash my wife had tied
        as I departed?
Unless it tears itself apart
    it will stay there till we meet

112.

These arms were used
    to hold my lovely wife
        as we slept entwined
How could they ever again
    pillow another woman's head?

113.

When I am awake
    I cannot speak of such things
        but in my dreams
I can see myself asleep
    pillowed by my lover's sleeves

114.

Drifting deeply
 snow is blown by the wind
  on this cold night
While I wonder if my love
 must also sleep alone

115.

A range of mountains
    separates me from my love
        on this moonlit night
Yet, perhaps she's gone outside
    and stands in longing for me

116.

So late last night
    out into the dismal dark
        you sent me away
Please don't send me back tonight
    along that very long road

117.

I have entwined
    the threads of my life into
        a true lover's knot
So another time I'm sure
    I shall see you once again

118.

Perhaps a strong man
    should not offer love without
      having love returned
But this grieving ugly warrior
    still finds his love is growing

119.

Like a crying child
    who grasps at his mother's sleeves
      and pulls her back
I have just been cast aside
    and feel helpless in my plight

120.

Upon your leaving
    I would have that stretching road
      rolled and folded up
And burned to destruction—
    had I but flames from heaven!

121.

Once I did believe
   myself to be a warrior
     though I have found
Love has caused me to grow thin
     since my love was not returned

123.

Although I have heard
    that you were a gallant man
        you gave me no bed
You made me go home again
    oh, what a dullard gallant!

122.

My longing for her
    is a thousand waves that roll
        from the sea each day
Why is it so difficult
    to clasp that jewel to my wrist?

125.

Should you refuse me
    do you think I would force you?
    no, I would remain
Confused in love as roots of rush
    and still keep longing for you

124.

Yes, I was indeed
    a gallant man toward you
    I gave you no bed
Since I sent you home again
    I remain a gallant man

126.

Blooming here alone
    in this thick field of summer
    a single lily
Oh, how one can suffer so
    when his love is not known

127.

Instead of longing
    for my loved one in this way
    I would rather be
A jewel that could be clasped
    tightly to my lover's wrist

128.

Forced to stay away
    and love you from a distance
    I would rather be
The wild duck that I hear dwells
    at the lake beside your home

129.

Rather than to love
    with a love as dear as life
    and feel such longing
I would rather change into
    the tiller on my lover's boat

130.

Instead of suffering
    this longing for my loved one
    I would rather choose
To become a stone or tree
    without feelings or sad thoughts

131.

Although every year
    the plum bursts in bloom again
    I live in a world
Hollow as a locust shell
    where spring does not return

132.

To love someone
    who does not return that love
        is like offering prayers
Back behind a starving god
    within a Buddhist temple

133.

The things you told me
    were said to stave off silence
        and to console me
When I came to know the truth
    oh, the bitterness I felt!

134.

Using fine pillars
    of the highest grade cypress
        does the woodsman
Fabricate in wasted haste
    a mere temporary hut?

135.

It is fortunate
    for any man who can
        live so long to hear
The sound of his wife's voice
    till his black hair turns to white

136.

If from your mouth
    there hung a hundred-year-old tongue
        and you would babble
I still would not cease to care
    but indeed my love would grow

NOTES ON THE POEMS AND POETS

Note: Numbers that begin each entry refer to numbers assigned to the poems in this volume. Numbers immediately following in parentheses refer to the numbering of the poems in the *Kokka Taika (Conspectus of National Poetry)*, and are the same as the numbering in any standard Japanese language edition of the *Manyoshu*. The names of the poets given in the notes correspond to the names in the Nippon Gakujutsu Shin Kokai, *The Manyoshu: One Thousand Poems Selected and Translated from the Japanese with Text in Romaji and an Introduction, Notes, Maps, Biographical Notes, Chronological Tables, Etc.*, (New York: Columbia University Press, 1965).

1. (995) Poem by Lady Otomo of Sakanoé (eighth century). One of the finest women poets of the *Manyoshu*, she is represented by a total of eighty-four poems in the anthology. Born as the half sister of Otomo Tabito [see note 3], she later became aunt of Otomo Yakamochi [see note 2], who is often considered to be one of the chief editors of the *Manyoshu*. Married to another member of the Otomo clan, a family known for its military leadership, stretching back to the mythological age, she gave birth to a daughter also known for her poetry, who was called Otomo of Sakanoé's Elder Daughter [see note 13]. Later, this Elder Daughter married her own cousin, the famed Otomo Yakamochi, thus making Lady Otomo, Yakamochi's mother-in-law, as well as his aunt.

2. (469) Poem by Otomo Yakamochi (716-785), who is one of the most important poets of the *Manyoshu* and probably one of the last compilers of the work. Born the son of Otomo Tabito [see note 3] and the nephew of Lady Otomo of Sakanoé [see note 1], his early childhood contained an atmosphere of poetry fostered by the gatherings of his father's aristocratic poet friends. The *Manyoshu* contains nearly five hundred of Yakamochi's poems, all of which were probably written prior to his forty-second year. Most of his later work is said to have been lost. Yakamochi devoted much of his poetic life to the writing and receiving of love poems. Numerous poems in this present collection were either written by him or to him by a number of highly-placed women poets of the Nara Court. Lady Ki [see note 8] and Lady Kasa [see note 11] seem to have been admirers of his. One could also suspect that he was secretly involved with his own aunt/mother-in-law, the Lady Otomo of Sakanoé [see poems 107 and 108].

3. (1542) Poem by Otomo Tabito (665-731). Father of Otomo Yakamochi [see note 2], Tabito can be credited with instilling deep literary interests in his son, as well as having composed more than eighty *Manyoshu* poems himself. After having held a number of high positions in the Nara Court, he spent several of his last official years as a governor-general of southern Japan on the island of Kyushu, during which time his wife died. While on official duty in Kyushu, he gathered about him a group of outstanding scholars and poets of the time, including the famed Yamanoé Okura [see

note 39], and his own son, who was a teenager at the time. Like most learned gentlemen of the period, Tabito composed verse in the international language of China as well as in Japanese. His thirteen poems in praise of saké are favorites of *Manyoshu* readers and translators.

4. (1833)   Anonymous.

5. (1782)   Poem attributed to Kakinomoto Hitomaro [see note 58].

6. (1908)   Anonymous.

7. (399)   Poem by Fujiwara Yatsuka (died 765). Like Otomo Tabito, Yatsuka held the position of governor-general in Kyushu after an illustrious career in the Imperial Court in Nara.

8. (1452)   Poem by Lady Ki (eighth century). Daughter of Ki Kahito, who produced three *Manyoshu* poems himself, her given name was Ojika. She has twelve poems included in the anthology, five of which are love poems addressed to Otomo Yakamochi [see note 2] suggesting an early love affair between them before she became the consort of Prince Aki, the grandson of Emperor Tenji (reigned 664-671).

9. (695)   Poem by Princess Hirokawa (eighth century), a great granddaughter of the Emperor Temmu (reigned 673-686).

10. (1915)   Anonymous.

11. (1451)   Poem by Lady Kasa (eighth century). Except for approximately twenty poems that she wrote professing love for Otomo Yakamochi [see note 2], little is known about this woman or her family. Since Yakamochi replied little to her pleas for attention, it can be presumed that the love was one-sided, leaving Lady Kasa with feelings of deep despair and longing [see poems 26, 29, 38, 56, and 132].

12. (3757)   Anonymous.

13. (735)   Poem by Lady Otomo of Sakanoé's Elder Daughter (eighth century) [see note 2].

14. (1876)   Anonymous.

15. (1211)   Anonymous.

16. (710)   Poem by Lady Ato Tobira (eighth century).

17. (3580)   Anonymous.

18. (1909)   Anonymous.

19. (584)   Poem by Lady Otomo of Sakanoé's Elder Daughter [see note 1]. This poem was a reply to a poem from Otomo Yakamochi [see note 2].

20. (632)   Poem by Prince Yuhara (eighth century). Considered by some scholars to be the second son of Prince Shiki, another poet of the *Manyoshu*, Prince Yuhara was therefore grandson of the Emperor Tenji (reigned 664-671). Although little is known about Yuhara, he does seem to have been closely associated with Otomo Yakamochi [see note 2]. In this poem to a young woman, the poet alludes to a Chinese legend concerning laurel believed to be growing on the moon.

21. (1897)   Anonymous.

22. (1394)   Anonymous.

23. (2239)   Anonymous.

24. (961)   Poem by Otomo Tabito [see note 3].

25. (1000)   Poem by Prince Moribe (eighth century), who was the grandson of Emperor Temmu (reigned 673-686) and the son of Prince Toneri (died 735). Prince Toneri was the compiler of the *Nihonshoki (Chronicles of*

Japan), which was completed in the year 720, but little is known about Prince Moribe himself.

26. (592) Poem by Lady Kasa [see note 11]. This poem is one of approximately twenty written by her and addressed to Otomo Yakamochi [see note 2].

27. (390) Poem by Princess Ki (eighth century), who was the daughter of the Emperor Temmu (reigned 673-686).

28. (782) Poem by Lady Ki [see note 8].

29. (604) Poem by Lady Kasa [see note 11] and addressed to Otomo Yakamochi [see note 2].

30. (625) Poem by Prince Takayasu (died 742). Little is known about this poet except that he held a number of appointments at court.

31. (3641) Anonymous.

32. (1726) Poem by Tajihi Mahito. Nothing is known about him.

33. (1727) Poem by an unknown fishing girl in answer to the preceding poem.

34. (1039) Poem by Takaoka Kochi, (eighth century). Little is known about this poet outside of his various court ranks. This poem shows one of the *Manyoshu*'s characteristic poetic techniques of writing from a loved one's point of view.

35. (1085) Anonymous.

36. (1925) Anonymous.

37. (1894) Anonymous.

38. (603) Poem by Lady Kasa [see note 11]. This is another of her poems to Otomo Yakamochi [see note 2].

39. (896) Poem by Yamanoé Okura (660?-733?). One of the most noteworthy poets of the *Manyoshu*, his style and tone appear unique. Growing up without parents, he seems to have suffered hardship as a child, and his longer poems on children and the poor are unforgettable. He did, however, gain access to the Nara Court and even journeyed to China as an official representative of the Japanese emperor. Later, after his return from China, he served as tutor to the crown prince. Following this period of service he was sent to Kyushu where he held a position of political importance under Otomo Tabito [see note 3] and became involved with the poetry circle that formed under Tabito's leadership. Okura also composed poetry and prose in Chinese, as was fashionable for the learned men of his time.

40. (1518) Poem by Yamanoé Okura [see note 39]. In this poem he alludes to the Chinese legend about the weaving girl and the herdsman who were forced to live on opposing sides of the Milky Way. The two lovers were permitted one meeting a year, an event still said to take place on the evening of the seventh day of the seventh month of the year.

41. (4321) Poem by Mononobe Akimochi (eighth century). Mononobe was the poet's clan name. He probably served as a frontier guard, since his clan is known to have provided such military service for the Imperial Court.

42. (4343) Poem by Tamatsukuribe Hirome (eighth century), who has a frontier guard.

43. (4333) Poem by Otomo Yakamochi [see note 2].

44. (439) Poem by Otomo Tabito [see note 3]. One of several poems addressed to the poet's dead wife.

45. (636)   Poem by Prince Yuhara [see note 20].

46. (637)   Poem by an anonymous woman written in reply to Prince Yuhara's poem above. Some scholars believe the woman was his wife.

47. (4431)   Poem by Iware Morokimi (eighth century).

48. (4351)   Poem by Tamatsukuribe Kunioshi (eighth century), a frontier guard.

49. (4420)   Poem by Kurahashibe Otome (eighth century), a young wife who in this poem expresses her wish that no other woman do her husband's mending while he is away on frontier guard duty.

50. (3717)   Anonymous.

51. (4424)   Poem by Lady Mononobe Tojime, a frontier guard's wife.

52. (1692)   Anonymous.

53. (1479)   Poem by Otomo Yakamochi [see note 2].

54. (1982)   Anonymous.

55. (1663)   Poem by Otomo Yakamochi [see note 2].

56. (607)   Poem by Lady Kasa [see note 11]. Another poem to Otomo Yakamochi [see note 2].

57. (3747)   Anonymous.

58. (497)   Poem by Kakinomoto Hitomaro (late seventh and early eighth century). Known to posterity as the "Saint of Poetry," he is considered to be the greatest of all poets represented in the *Manyoshu*. Hundreds of his poems have been preserved in the anthology, yet little is known about the man himself except what can be learned from his poetry. He was active in court circles before the capital city of Nara was established, where he seems to have served as an official poet laureate to at least two emperors.

59. (498)   Poem by Kakinomoto Hitomaro [see note 58]. The poet replies in verse to the question posed in the preceding poem.

60. (690)   Poem by Otomo Miyori (died 774). Very little is known about this man except for his court ranks and the position he held as governor of several provinces. On one occasion of official service, he served under Otomo Tabito [see note 3] and probably joined in the poetry activities under his direction.

61. (1995)   Anonymous.

62. (2244)   Anonymous.

63. (3746)   Anonymous.

64. (2201)   Anonymous.

65. (1606)   Poem by Princess Nukada (seventh century). The dates of her life are unknown, but she is considered to be one of the leading women poets of the *Manyoshu*. The Emperor Temmu (reigned 673-686) considered her a favorite, and she gave birth to an Imperial princess.

66. (1271)   Poem attributed to Kakinomoto Hitomaro [see note 58].

67. (1788)   Poem attributed to Kasa Kanamura (eighth century). The *Manyoshu* contains at least four previously existing anthologies: the *Hitomaro*, the *Kanamura*, the *Mushimaro*, and the *Sakimaro* Collections. Scholars are not sure if the poetry included in these Collections was written by the men whose names are associated with them, or if the poems included were merely collected by the named poets. This poem appears in the *Kanamura* Collection and may or may not have been written by the poet himself. Little of interest is known about the man.

68. (1078) Anonymous.

69. (1607) Poem by Princess Kagami (seventh century), sister of Princess Nukada [see note 65]. This poem was apparently written at the same time as the poem of Princess Nukada.

70. (1541) Poem by Otomo Tabito [see note 3].

71. (1609) Poem by Tajihi Mahito (eighth century). Nothing is known about the man.

72. (1611) Poem by Princess Kasanui (seventh or eighth century). Little is known about this woman.

73. (953) Poem attributed both to Kasa Kanamura [see note 67], and to Kuramochi Chitose (eighth century), of whom little is known.

74. (1613) Poem attributed to Princess Kamo (seventh or eighth century).

75. (1511) Poem by the Emperor Jomei (reigned 629-641).

76. (493) Poem by Tabe Ichiiko, of whom little is known.

77. (124) Poem by the daughter of Sono Ikuha (seventh or early eighth century). Nothing is known about this woman.

78. (1924) Anonymous.

79. (4302) Poem by Okisome Hase (eighth century).

80. (1777) Poem by someone known only as "A Young Woman of Harima" (eighth century).

81. (3669) Anonymous.

82. (4322) Poem by Wakayamatobe Mumaro (eighth century), a frontier guard.

83. (1367) Anonymous.

84. (462) Poem by Otomo Yakamochi [see note 2].

85. (3713) Anonymous.

86. (4301) Poem by Lord Asukabe (eighth century).

87. (2241) Anonymous.

88. (3639) Anonymous.

89. (1620) Poem by Lady Otomo of Sakanoé [see note 1]. This poem was written to Otomo Yakamochi [see note 2].

90. (741) Poem by Otomo Yakamochi [see note 2]. This was one of fifteen poems he sent to Lady Otomo of Sakanoé's Elder Daughter [see note 1].

91. (463) Poem by Otomo Fumimochi (eighth century), the younger brother of Yakamochi. No other particulars are known about him.

92. (440) Poem by Otomo Tabito [see note 3]. In this poem he again recalls his wife who died in Kyushu.

93. (2237) Anonymous.

94. (1573) Poem by Otomo Toshikami (eighth century).

95. (88) Poem by Empress Iwa-no-hime (died 347). She was the Empress-consort of the Emperor Nintoku (reigned 313-399). Many poems are said to have been exchanged between them. The present one is said to have been written in longing while the Emperor was away on a journey.

96. (1702) Anonymous.

97. (2129) Anonymous.

98. (1562) Poem by Lady Kannagibe Maso (eighth century). Nothing is known about her, although some sources suggest that she may have been a "vestal virgin" associated with a shrine. The poem itself appears to have been written to Otomo Yakamochi [see note 2].

99. (1563) Poem by Otomo Yakamochi [see note 2]. This poem is intended to be a reply to the poem directly above and seems to indicate his resentment of the lady's cloistered existence.

100. (1567) Poem by Otomo Yakamochi [see note 2].

101. (1574) Anonymous.

102. (2240) Anonymous.

103. (1515) Poem by Princess Tajima (died 708), who was the daughter of Emperor Temmu (reigned 673-686).

104. (1983) Anonymous.

105. (730) Poem by Lady Otomo of Sakanoé's Elder Daughter [see note 1] to Otomo Yakamochi [see note 2].

106. (1992) Anonymous.

107. (683) Poem by Lady Otomo of Sakanoé [see note 1].

108. (728) Poem by Otomo Yakamochi [see note 2] to Lady Otomo of Sakanoé [see note 1].

109. (2243) Anonymous.

110. (468) Poem by Otomo Yakamochi [see note 2].

111. (1789) Poem attributed to Kasa Kanamura [see note 67].

112. (438) Poem by Otomo Tabito [see note 3]. Again, he recalls his wife who died in Kyushu.

113. (784) Poem by Otomo Yakamochi [see note 2], written to an unknown woman.

114. (59) Poem by Lady Yosa. Nothing is known about her.

115. (765) Poem by Otomo Yakamochi [see note 2] to Lady Otomo of Sakanoé's Elder Daughter [see note 13].

116. (781) Poem by Otomo Yakamochi [see note 2] to Lady Ki [see note 8].

117. (763) Poem by Lady Ki [see note 8] to Otomo Yakamochi [see note 2].

118. (117) Poem by Prince Toneri (died 735). The learned son of the Emperor Temmu (reigned 673-686), he compiled the *Nihonshoki (Chronicles of Japan)* in the year 720.

119. (492) Poem by Tabe Ichiiko [see note 76].

120. (3724) Poem by Lady Sano. Little is known about her.

121. (719) Poem by Otomo Yakamochi [see note 2].

122. (409) Poem by Otomo Sukunamaro (eighth century), husband of Lady Otomo of Sakanoé [see note 1] and father of Lady Otomo of Sakanoé's Elder Daughter [see note 13].

123. (126) Poem by Lady Ishikawa (seventh or eighth century). Nothing is known about her except for the following story:
Lady Ishikawa admired the handsome courtier Otomo Tanushi [see note 124]. She desired to bring some attention to herself, but could not think of a proper plan. Finally, she disguised herself as an old peasant woman and paid a call upon Tanushi under the pretext of asking for fire. She hoped, of course, that he would discover her trickery and invite her to spend the night. Instead, he

91

merely gave her a bucket of embers and sent her on her way. The next day, indignant and frustrated, she sent him the poem included here.

124. (127) Poem by Otomo Tanushi (seventh or eighth century). The "gallant" younger brother brother of Otomo Tabito [see note 3].

125. (679) Poem by Lady Nakatomi (eighth century). Except for several poems written to Otomo Yakamochi [see note 2], nothing is known about her.

126. (1500) Poem by Lady Otomo of Sakanoé [see note 1].

127. (734) Poem by Otomo Yakamochi [see note 2] to Lady Otomo of Sakanoé [see note 1].

128. (726) Poem by Lady Otomo of Sakanoé [see note 1]. This poem was offered to the Emperor Shomu (reigned 724-749) who, being an ardent Buddhist, established monasteries throughout the country and was responsible for starting construction of the Great Buddha of Nara.

129. (1455) Poem by Kasa Kanamura [see note 67].

130. (722) Poem by Otomo Yakamochi [see note 2].

131. (1857) Anonymous.

132. (608) Poem by Lady Kasa [see note 11] to Otomo Yakamochi [see note 2].

133. (1258) Anonymous.

134. (1355) Anonymous.

135. (1411) Anonymous.

136. (764) Poem by Otomo Yakamochi [see note 2] to Lady Ki [see note 8].

CREDITS

All illustrations listed in this book are Japanese in origin.

Cover: Doves and Rhododendrons (detail), two-panel screen, gold and colors on paper, late seventeenth century. Courtesy of The Art Institute of Chicago.

Page 14. Two Poems on the Subject of the Moon, Man'yoshu, Book VII, style of Fujiwara no Yoshitsune (1169-1206), mounted as a hanging scroll, originally in book form, ink and pale red ink on paper. Courtesy of the Fogg Art Museum, Harvard University, anonymous loan. The poems translate:

> [1] I am not one/usually concerned so much/over the moon/Yet, it shall sink from our sight/filling the night with longing

> [2] Brandishing long bows/a band of stalwart men/hunt in the hills/Even the distant fields below/are clearly seen by moonlight

Page 17. Plum branch, attributed to Suzuki Nanrei (1775-1884). The Harari Collection, London.

Page 19. A waterfall, Hara Zaichu (1750-1837). The Harari Collection, London.

Page 20. Full moon over tree-tops, Ito Jakuchu (1716-1800). The Harari Collection, London.

Page 23. Splashed ink landscape, Shukei Sesson, ink on paper, Muromachi Period, mid-sixteenth century. Courtesy of the Denver Art Museum, Denver, Colorado.

Page 25. Narihira Riding below Fuji, Sakai Hoitsu, ca. 1820, ink and color on silk. Courtesy of The Minneapolis Institute of Arts, Bequest of Richard P. Gale.

Pages 26-27. White egret on a wave, anonymous, Kano School, Kakemono, ink on paper, mid-Edo Period. Honolulu Academy of Arts, gift of Mrs. Charles M. Cooke, Sr., 1929.

Page 28. "Poem," with birds in flight, Nonomura Sotatsu (1576-1643), and Honnami Koetsu (1558-1637). Nelson Gallery—Atkins Museum, Kansas City, Missouri, gift of George H. Bunting, Jr.

Pages 30-31. Plovers and Beached Boat, Shibata Zeshin (1807-1891), *Album of Twelve Fan Paintings,* lacquer on paper. Seattle Art Museum, Eugene Fuller Memorial Collection.

Page 32. A fishing party, Suzuki Harunobu, chuban color-print, eighteenth century. Courtesy of The Minneapolis Institute of Arts, Bequest of Richard P. Gale.

Page 34. Landscape: early summer, Ogata Korin (1658-1716), twofold screen, ink and gold on paper. Seattle Art Museum, Thomas D. Stimson Memorial Collection.

Page 37. Seascape with Gulls and Waves, Shibata Zeshin (1807-1891), *Album of Twelve Fan Paintings,* lacquer on paper. Seattle Art Museum, Eugene Fuller Memorial Collection.

Page 38. A girl standing beneath a flower arrangement, Miyagawa Issho, eighteenth century. Courtesy of The Minneapolis Institute of Arts, Bequest of Richard P. Gale.

Page 41. Standing beauty with sleeve to her mouth, artist unknown, ca. 1650, ink and color on paper. Courtesy of The Minneapolis Institute of Arts, Bequest of Richard P. Gale.

Pages 44-45. Court girl unrolling bamboo blind, Keii Hironaga, eighteenth century. The Harari Collection, London.

Page 47. Tree in mist, attributed to Suzuki Nanrei (1775-1804). The Harari Collection, London.

Page 49. Sparrow and rice-ear, Kameoka Kirei (1770-1835). The Harari Collection, London.

Page 51. Rider and attendant in snow, nineteenth century. The Art Gallery of Greater Victoria.

Page 52. Bamboo and a full moon, So Gyokurin, nineteenth century. The Harari Collection, London.

Page 54. Wild deer, Mori Tetsuzan, ca. 1815, ink and color on paper. Courtesy of The Minneapolis Institute of Arts, Bequest of Richard P. Gale.

Page 56. Sanjurokkasen (Thirty-Six Poets), unknown, album, color and gold on paper, seventeenth to eighteenth centuries. From the Permanent Collection of the Art Gallery of Greater Victoria.

Page 60. Summer and autumn grasses (detail), Sakai Hoitsu (1761-1828), twofold screen, color on silk. Seattle Art Museum, Eugene Fuller Memorial Collection.

Page 63. Swallows and waves, Okamoto Shuki (1785-1862). Shinenkan Collection.

Page 67. Flying goose, Yosen-in Korenobu (1753-1808). The Harari Collection, London.

Page 68. Dish with design of three wild geese in flight, Nezumi Shino ware, ca. 1600. The Cleveland Museum of Art, gift of Mrs. A. Dean Perry.

Page 70. Young man playing a shoulder drum, Tsunemasa, ca. 1750, ink and color on silk. Courtesy of The Minneapolis Institute of Arts, Bequest of Richard P. Gale.

Page 74. Fisherman carrying his net in the snow, Katsushika Hokusai, ca. 1821, ink and color on paper. Courtesy of The Minneapolis Institute of Arts, Bequest of Richard P. Gale.

Page 77. Sword guard with dragon and waves, Issan, nineteenth century. The Cleveland Museum of Art, gift of D. Z. Norton.

Pages 78-79. Wave screen, attributed to Ogata Korin (1658-1716), six-panel screen, ink, blue and gold on paper. Seattle Art Museum, Eugene Fuller Memorial Collection.

Page 83. A flock of rooks, Kusumi Morikage, ca. 1700, ink on paper. Courtesy of The Minneapolis Institute of Arts, Bequest of Richard P. Gale.

Photograph by R. D. Turoff, 1979

Harold Wright, currently a professor of Asian Studies at Antioch College, has spent many years in Japan studying and translating Japanese poetry. He has been the recipient of a Fulbright Fellowship, a Ford Foundation Fellowship, the Columbia University Translation Center Prize, and a National Translation Center Award.

This book was set in linotype Janson by the
Jackson Typesetting Company, Jackson, Michigan.

Printed and bound by The Haddon Craftsmen, Inc.,
Scranton, Pennsylvania.

Photo research by Angela Gwynn.

Designed by Julia Runk and Hazel Bercholz.